T HE PROGRESSIVE LEFT understood the assignment: control the classroom, control the future. To instill collectivist values in America's children through public education, they have deployed benevolent-sounding phrases – like "Diversity, Equity, and Inclusion (DEI)." Although President Trump has declared war on DEI and this particular brand may fade, the fight is far from over.

Like a hydra, the collectivist beast has many heads. Terms like "Global Literacy," "Cultural Competence," and "Social Awareness" loom large in education today. Seemingly harmless, they share a common thread – they weaponize empathy, using emotional appeals to smuggle radical ideology into classrooms under colorful banners of compassion.

The most potent of them all? A tool called "Social Emotional Learning" (SEL).

While SEL sounds uncontroversial in

theory, in practice it "serves as a delivery mechanism for radical pedagogy, such as critical race theory and gender deconstructionism," says Manhattan Institute Senior Fellow Christopher Rufo, who has made it his mission to defeat DEI in all its forms.

The aim of SEL, Rufo argues, is to "soften children at an emotional level, reinterpret their normative behavior as an expression of repression, whiteness or internalized racism, and then rewire their behavior according to the dictates of left-wing ideology."

This broadside aims to expose SEL as the underlying architecture of the school-to-progressivism pipeline.

I. THE IDEOLOGICAL ENGINE OF SEL: FROM "EMPATHY" TO "EQUITY"

In the late 1960s, a young Harvard grad student boarded a plane to India. Dan Goleman had landed a traveling fellowship to study ancient systems of psychology and the meditation practices of Asian religions. What he

THE NEW FACE

OF

WOKE

EDUCATION

PRISCILLA WEST

 **ENCOUNTER** **N°** **71**
BROADSIDE

ENCOUNTER BROADSIDES

Inaugurated in the fall of 2009, Encounter Broadsides are a series of timely pamphlets and e-books from Encounter Books. Uniting an 18th century sense of public urgency and rhetorical wit (think The Federalist Papers, Common Sense*) with 21st century technology and channels of distribution, Encounter Broadsides offer indispensable ammunition for intelligent debate on the critical issues of our time. Written with passion by some of our most authoritative authors, Encounter Broadsides make the case for ordered liberty and the institutions of democratic capitalism at a time when they are under siege from the resurgence of collectivist sentiment. Read them in a sitting and come away knowing the best we can hope for and the worst we must fear.*

absorbed there, under the mentorship of spiritual guru Neem Karoli Baba, would reshape American education in ways that few could have predicted.

Inspired by spiritual leaders like the Dalai Lama, Goleman wrote several books on Eastern meditation "to render the exotic more familiar" for Westerners. In *The Meditative Mind* he recalled, "I remember the late Tibetan teacher Chögyam Trungpa telling me in 1974, *'Buddhism will come to the West as a psychology.'*"

Indeed, by 1995 Goleman published the best-selling *Emotional Intelligence*, which subtly wove Eastern spiritual concepts into a scientific framework for a Western audience. His work was funded by the Fetzer Institute – a New Age spiritualist organization – and heavily promoted by *The New York Times*,

---

Like a hydra, the collectivist beast has many heads.

---

where Goleman worked as a science reporter. The book launched a movement so expertly wreathed in secular academic jargon that even its practitioners often don't recognize its metaphysical origins.

The Fetzer Institute's mission, "helping build the spiritual foundation for a loving world" was not directly applicable to American public schools. So instead, Goleman – along with Fetzer official David Sluyter, Roger Weissberg, Eileen Rockefeller, Timothy Shriver, and others – formed a new entity called CASEL (Collaborative for Advancement of Social Emotional Learning) at the Yale Child Study Center. Recast as neutral forms of "intelligence" and "learning," CASEL's (and Fetzer's) decidedly non-academic ideals could be pushed wholesale into American schools.

It was at a Fetzer-hosted conference in 1994 that the new educational mission field got its name – "Social Emotional Learning."

Social Emotional Learning ostensibly nurtures the "whole child" by teaching students to process emotions, set goals, build relationships, and make smart choices in school and life. It looks different from state to state, and school to school. One teacher might lead SEL lessons during "circle time" prompting students to share feelings about personal experiences. Another may have each child point to their "feelings zone" on an "emotional thermometer." Some schools request emotional "check-ins" using an app. Self-reflection activities like journaling and surveys are common – as are breathing exercises and video broadcasts on SEL topics.

By 1997, the architects of woke curricula at CASEL had coauthored the first book on school-based SEL programming. The seminal work, *Promoting Social and Emotional Learning: Guidelines for Educators*, formally defined SEL as:

> *The process of acquiring and effectively applying the knowledge, attitudes, and skills necessary to recognize and manage emotions; developing caring and concern for others; making responsible decisions; establishing positive relationships;*

and handling challenging situations capably.
(Elias, et al., 1997)

Sounds great, right?

Within five years of creating the field, CASEL's *Safe and Sound* guide reviewed a remarkable 80– *eighty!* – "nationally available, multiyear, sequenced [SEL] programs" and helped build credibility for SEL among policymakers. CASEL worked with the Illinois State Board of Education to develop the first statewide SEL standards in the nation, aligned with CASEL's five competencies (self-awareness, self-management, social awareness, relationship skills, and responsible decision-making.) Illinois officially adopted the standards in 2004, and SEL was off to the races. Lawmakers were sold on the notion that these so-called "non-cognitive skills" should be cultivated by the school system.

Parents too, were optimistic. After all, who wouldn't want their kids to manage emotions, make responsible decisions, and have positive relationships? McGraw Hill Education, a major player in the industry, produced a survey claiming that nearly four out of five of parents say SEL skills should be taught in the classroom. This parental support, however, was gauged *after* McGraw Hill supplied parents with a CASEL-inspired definition of SEL.

CASEL's influence grew. CASEL psychologists' prolific research and publications became the bedrock of a multibillion-dollar industry churning out teacher training, curricula, parent resources, and – most essentially – classroom software.

As learning moved into the cloud, edtech providers began beaming subscription-based coursework directly into classrooms. Some focused primarily on SEL, like Panorama Education which was already reaching 10 percent of American students by 2017 and EverFi which partnered with the National Football League to offer its "Character Playbook" software free to schools in all 32 NFL markets. Others, like textbook titans Pearson (now Savvas Learning) and McGraw Hill built

SEL into core academic subjects – all citing CASEL as the gold standard.

Publisher Houghton Mifflin Harcourt was explicit: "SEL is infused throughout our evidence-based literacy, math, social studies, and science programs. It's incorporated in whole-class and small-group instructional resources, collaborative and student-choice activities, and personalized feedback delivered by adaptive software."

Before the COVID pandemic, parents had sensed unsettling changes in their children's classrooms. But when 2020 school closures sent learning home to the kitchen table, they saw firsthand how the lessons had been politicized. Exercises like "My Many Identities" in the "Welcoming Schools" program from the Human Rights Campaign – which prompts even kindergarteners to ponder questions of race, class, and gender identity – sparked scrutiny.

The architects of this transformation had deep pockets. In the decade before the pandemic, venture capital groups such as the

CASEL psychologists' prolific research and publications became the bedrock of a multibillion-dollar industry churning out teacher training, curricula, parent resources, and — most essentially — classroom software.

Chan Zuckerberg Initiative and the Emerson Collective, and major foundations including Gates, Kellogg, Allstate, and Wallace, all poured hundreds of millions into digital SEL resources and curricula. Even with positive slogans about "empowering youth," or "advancing equity," it was becoming apparent to some that SEL weaponizes education against American and family values.

Now, busy parents trying to understand SEL urgently needed to decode decades of progressive academic literature and the centuries of political philosophy behind it. Reflecting on that time, Florida mom Crystal Marull recalled, "There I was listening to a four-hour podcast on esoteric academic theory in one ear, [while] checking the kids' spelling words and handing out juice boxes."

Once SEL was embedded deeply into American schooling, CASEL moved the goalposts. It changed both the definition of SEL *and* its framework. Children forced into online schooling by the 2020 school closures imbibed an SEL more toxic than the original version. The "official" definition had doubled in length and ambiguity, now including progressive concepts like "healthy identities," "collective goals," and "just communities." This shifted the focus from self-management to political consciousness.

The result? Newer SEL versions openly encourage social justice activism. A 2020 United Nations Educational, Scientific and Cultural Organization (UNESCO) publication called "SEL & Activism" featured this quote by Sabaah Folayan, "Don't wait for permission to be an activist. Don't ask for forgiveness, either." In Illinois, 13-year-old Rashad Evans credited SEL for his participation in a Black Lives Matter protest, telling CASEL summit attendees, "Our generation has to take a stand...and if we unite now, we will be unstoppable." CASEL President Karen Niemi affirmed in "SEL as a Lever for Equity and Social Justice" that SEL helps people "move from anger, to agency, and then to *action*." Notably absent was any discussion of how school children might be guided toward such anger in the first place – or who might benefit from putting them there.

In 2021, the American Federation of Teachers approvingly quoted a new CASEL resource, saying it will "[redistribute] power to promote social justice through increased engagement in school and civic life." The following year, the ideological shift was on full display when the National Education Association began promoting Black Lives Matter at School's Week of Action. As part of the program, the kindergarten and first grade team of Denver's Centennial Elementary School rolled out "transgender affirming" lessons and a rejection of "Western nuclear family dynamics" in favor of the "collective village."

Yet even as SEL evolved from empathy to equity, its public justifications remain largely technocratic. Dan Goleman helped "sciencify" the movement in the 1990s mapping "emotional intelligence" onto brain structures like the amygdala and the prefrontal cortex. Today, the discourse is peppered with references to brain scans and neuroplasticity. A 2021 UNESCO report *Building Kinder Brains* is emblematic, invoking "neuroscience" to claim that SEL "provides a double dividend to learners and society by improving academic achievements and...building a kinder world." John Fetzer and Chögyam Trungpa would be proud.

SEL is presented as a values-neutral, scientifically grounded, "soft skills" upgrade to education. But it is really a specific worldview formation. Sold to parents, teachers, and policymakers as a benign supplement for "emotional intelligence," it became a means of ideological indoctrination.

SEL's metaphysical and ideological origins might have remained confined to academic circles – if not for a parallel revolution in education that enabled SEL to be digitized, tracked, and enforced at scale.

II. From Mindfulness to Metrics: DEI in the District

In April 2024, a US federal judge awarded $2.6 million to Chicago students who were coerced into participating in Hindu worship rituals between 2015 and 2019. Muslim plaintiff Kaya Hudgins testified that the sessions "felt like hypnosis or being in a trance." Nothing to see here – just state-funded transcendental meditation, innocuously called "Quiet Time" by Chicago Public Schools.

That was the old SEL. Since the 2020 CASEL "updates," school board meetings and social media are flooded with troubling examples of how the newer, identity-focused SEL is playing out in America's classrooms. "Resilience" lessons are often "trauma-informed," recasting misbehavior as response to racial inequity or unmet emotional needs. "Affinity groups" and "Identity circles" separate students based on race, ethnicity, or sexual orientation. Even more insidious, DEI-style

---

Once SEL was embedded deeply into American schooling, CASEL moved the goalposts.

---

struggle sessions often escape scrutiny – either because they happen within online learning platforms, or they're shielded by a culture of confidentiality, reinforced with mantras like "What is said in the circle stays in the circle."

How did we get here?

It turns out that "Common Core" – a controversial Obama-era reform effort to align

K-12 learning standards nationwide – was not just a passing fad in education. And the parallel rise of SEL and Common Core was no accident. As Common Core nationalized testing and integrated data systems, SEL began tracking students along social and emotional dimensions. Both movements were fueled by global figures such as Bill Gates, Mark Zuckerberg, and Warren Buffett. Influential players saw the power of framing socio-emotional attributes as "skills" – and embedding them into new, *nationwide* learning standards – to effect sweeping social change.

Back in 2010, the insertion of soft skills into the Common Core State Standards (CCSS) opened the door for previously unthinkable system-wide student psychometric assessment. The CCSS math standard, for example, required students to "make sense of problems and persevere in solving them." As such, schools would now not only grade a student's work for accuracy, but they would also assess his level of *perseverance.* Likewise, the CCSS English Language Arts standard stressed *collaboration*, ushering in SEL topics like "social awareness."

A 2015 joint study by CASEL and the University of Texas at Austin referred to learning as a "social process" and said "Common Core State Standards for Mathematical Practice and (SEL) competencies are inextricably linked." CASEL board member Maurice Elias even said that "Common Core has an implicit dependence on SEL-related pedagogy."

Why was Common Core designed this way? The recasting of social-emotional traits as "academic" standards meant that they could be tracked alongside reading and math scores. And since classroom teachers could not be reasonably expected to measure students' psychological capacities, private corporations created sophisticated platforms for SEL assessment and analysis.

Panorama Education Inc., founded by a group of Yale students including the son-in-law of Attorney General Merrick Garland, is a top competitor in this space. Panorama raised $80M in seed capital from the Chan

Zuckerberg Initiative and likeminded venture capitalists including the Emerson Collective (Laurene Jobs), Sundar Pichai (Google), and Sam Altman (OpenAI). As one Panorama founder explained, it was the potential *social impact*, not just financial return, that got Mark Zuckerberg's attention.

Panorama deals in "soft skills." It measures so-called "competencies" such as "self-awareness" and empathy. It conducts student surveys and "check-ins" and offers behavior logging and analytics. It also allows teachers to record observations about students' social struggles or emotional issues. This vignette by author Abigail Shrier nails the disturbing implications of SEL tracking: *"I'm just meeting you now, in the eleventh grade, but it says here'* — [click, click] — *'you and a cousin engaged in inappropriate touching in kindergarten. Would you like to talk about it?'"* Anchoring the business model, SEL platforms offer "solutions" for monitoring progress within "learning frameworks" created by entities like CASEL and the National School Climate Center. A framework is a structured set of goals – benchmarks for what students should know or be able to do at each stage of their development. Most major frameworks in use today – such as Multi-Tiered Systems of Support (MTSS) or Portrait of a Graduate–track SEL "skills" alongside academics and behavioral traits. Behavioral and emotional competencies are treated as definitive learning outcomes. Unlike reading or math however, their measurement is fraught with subjectivity and bias. Panorama Education to the rescue!

[*Editor's Note: The architecture of SEL's digital delivery system – including the learning frameworks and cloud-based software vendors tracking student emotions – will be unpacked in Part II of this series.*]

The global SEL market is estimated at $9 Billion, with the largest online SEL platforms handling the personal information of tens of millions of children. Among the most widely used are EverFi (45 million students), Second Step (26 million), and Panorama Education (15 million.) Nearly all of them, and the metrics they track, are "CASEL aligned."

Although "Diversity, Equity, and Inclusion" is increasingly controversial, the inculcation of a collectivist worldview continues apace via cloud-based e-learning platforms. Whatever the next incarnation of DEI, its *delivery system* remains deeply entrenched in the education apparatus. [Thanks to Common Core, it *is* the education apparatus.]

Behavioral and emotional competencies are treated as definitive learning outcomes. Unlike reading or math however, their measurement is fraught with subjectivity and bias.

III. SEL Morphology: Many Names, One Agenda

SEL wears many hats. After three decades, what began as programming for "emotional intelligence" can now be invoked by dozens of names. But as titles change, the agenda remains the same: Normalize the behavioral conditioning and psychological profiling of children and embed it into *everything* they do.

"21st Century Skills" (2001)

For a time in the early 2000s, SEL's "competencies" were folded into a broader framework of "21st Century Skills." Tech titans Microsoft, Dell, Cisco, Apple, and AOL joined with the National Education Association teachers' union and the US Department of Education to form the public-private Partnership for 21st Century Skills (P21). Their goal was realized in 2007 when President George W. Bush's "America Competes Act" called for state data gathering on "21st century learning skills" including "critical thinking," "collaboration," and "global awareness."

Today, Panorama Education Inc. defines 21st Century Skills even more broadly, as "knowledge, life skills, career skills, habits, and traits that are critically important to student success in today's world, particularly as students move on to college, the workforce, and adult life."

"Common Core" (*2010*)

Like 21st Century Skills, the Common Core was engineered through public-private partnership. The Bill and Melinda Gates Foundation was the primary financial backer, funding Achieve, Inc., the National Governors Association, and the Council of Chief State School Officers throughout the design and rollout. Notably, all three are private entities – not government agencies – despite names suggesting otherwise. As such, they were not subject to Freedom of Information Act laws, even as they accepted private funding to rewire the national education infrastructure.

Common Core State Standards (CCSS) embedded the "21st Century Skills," prioritizing non-cognitive traits alongside academics. And while the academic benchmarks sparked debate, the related Common Education Data Standard quietly made student data systems interoperable across all 50 states.

Critics of the Common Core academic standards rightly objected to the emphasis of "soft skills" like "collaboration" at the cost of foundational knowledge. More alarming, though, is that hardwiring SEL into CCSS frameworks *digitized* the tracking of students' personal values, social and emotional traits.

"Global Citizenship" (*2012*)

In 2012, UNESCO launched its Global Citizenship Education (GCED) program to align schooling worldwide to the UN's sustainability agenda. GCED promotes themes like gender equality, cultural diversity, and environmental sustainability (see also: "Peace Education.") Student progress is tracked across three GCED-prescribed learning domains: cognitive, behavioral, and socio-emotional.

SEL may have begun as a stateside initiative, but it was scaled and spread through vehicles like the UN's GCED program. By embedding SEL into global frameworks, the UN flipped the script. Schools are not directly controlled by the UN, but they are often tied to state policies, accreditation standards, NGO partnerships, or grant requirements that cite UN goals. In this way, programs like GCED effectively enlist schools to advance global policy goals. The top-down structure doesn't just threaten local autonomy; it uses schools worldwide for a social engineering campaign that promotes collectivist values.

"Readiness" (mid-2010s)

As Common Core fell out of favor, "College and Career Readiness" became the new mantra. Each state crafted its own definition and signature mix of academic goals and SEL-style "workforce competencies" or "life skills."

As such, both academic and vocational tracks would now include student SEL metrics. What is more, the Workforce Data Quality Initiative (WDQI) – a collaborative effort by the Departments of Education and Labor – standardized and linked each individual's data from pre-K through college and the workforce.

Popular "readiness" frameworks include College, Career, and Life Readiness by Naviance, and Employability Skills by the US Department of Education. The models use vague, overlapping terms such as "life skills," "employability skills," and "workplace readiness." In addition to academic benchmarks, "readiness" models track the same types of non-academic, psycho-behavioral traits as SEL models.

Edtech firms like Naviance, YouScience, and Xello have carved niches in the "readiness" space. Their tools mimic SEL software – "employability" tests, "learning style" quizzes, personality profiles, and interest inventories – all handily synced with aca-

> *The district acknowledged that they had modified the language "to be in better alignment with the state board language" around mental health.*

demic and behavioral records for "whole child" analysis. Many school systems buy packages for grades K-12, prompting the question: Why are kindergartners – who could learn by visiting a farm, fire station, or film set – logging into "career exploration" modules?

"Resiliency" (Florida, 2022-)

By 2022, conservative backlash against SEL was gaining traction. Florida was home to the activist group Moms for Liberty, which educates parents about the divisive ideologies often embedded in SEL lessons. That year, the

FL Board of Education announced a pivot from its required mental health instruction to Resiliency Education. "Resilience" plays well with conservatives, who welcomed it as a move away from nonconsensual SEL interventions in schools.

Florida First Lady Casey DeSantis held a high-profile roundtable outlining the state's new $21 million framework for "resiliency skills" including grit, gratitude, personal responsibility, volunteerism, critical thinking, empathy, and citizenship.

But a closer look revealed little had changed. Pre-existing CASEL-aligned SEL programs in Hillsborough County, for instance, were simply renamed "resiliency, character, and life skills education." The district acknowledged that they had modified the language "to be in better alignment with the state board language" around mental health.

So, the question remains: What's the difference? Florida's "resilience" *sounds* apolitical, but its model overlaps with Common Core, SEL, and "readiness" – leaving parents to wonder how these skills will be measured. What kinds of student data is tracked to show improvements in "empathy" or "grit?"

Further, since all fifty states use a Common Educational Data Standard, do Florida's "resiliency" skills differ *at all* from CASEL's SEL competencies?

"Durable Skills" (North Carolina, 2024)

North Carolina is also piloting a new way to psychometrically profile school children. In October 2024, the US Department of Education awarded state educators in North Carolina a $4 million grant for "Durable Skills Assessment," by a Carnegie Foundation initiative called Skills for the Future.

The new assessments will target the (SEL) skills previously identified by North Carolina's "Portrait of a Graduate" framework: adaptability, collaboration, communication, critical thinking, empathy, learner's mindset, and personal responsibility. The state's commerce department (Labor Economic Analysis Division) stresses that these "durable skills" are "essential to every occupation in the state."

The head of the Carnegie initiative, Laura Slover, has a revealing background: she was Senior Vice President of Common Core initiator Achieve, Inc., CEO of a Common Core testing consortium, and a fellow at the Aspen Institute, which has received nearly $130 million from the Bill and Melinda Gates Foundation. Her appointment to lead the "Durable Skills" project once again highlights the links between Common Core and SEL.

Such measures risk elevating state-sanctioned "truth" over diverse viewpoints, further consolidating ideological control over public education.

Coursework in the so-called "new literacies" can also push globalist agendas. Learning frameworks that sidestep "empathy" or "equity" may instead tout "media literacy" or "global literacy," but these don't just rate research skills or geographic acumen. They really gauge acceptance of approved narratives. Dissent and be deemed "*illiterate.*"

One of the most widely used edtech platforms in American classrooms today is Newsela. It is a subscription-based news service that blends "media literacy" with English Language Arts and Social Studies. Launched in 2013 and heavily funded by Zuckerberg and the same venture capitalists who backed SEL platform development, Newsela purports to teach students how to evaluate news sources, recognize bias, and assess credibility. Today, the company reports reaching 40 million students in more than 90 percent of US K-12 schools.

In 2023, UNESCO's Media and Information Literacy Alliance teamed with Meta (Facebook) to combat so-called harmful content. Soon after, CEO Mark Zuckerberg testified that Biden officials had pressured him to censor alleged "disinformation."

These methods have even infiltrated science. Schools in 20 states have adopted "Next Generation Science Standards" (NGSS) which include climate change instruction aligned with the National Oceanic and Atmospheric Administration (NOAA) Climate Literacy framework. NOAA's "Climate Literacy" assumes impending man-made climate crisis and embraces "scientific consensus" alongside "Indigenous Knowledge" and "climate justice." And who oversaw the creation of NGSS? Common Core architect Achieve, Inc.

In 2022 the National Science Foundation awarded $1.2 million to Affectifi, Inc. to develop a web browser extension that integrates SEL with streaming sites to improve "emotional literacy... at scale." The same year,

NSF obligated $2.4 million – later increased to $5 million – to the University of Washington to "reimagine online information literacies" citing misinformation as a "growing threat to American democracy."

In the minefield of "new literacies," the age-old question arises: Who decides what is true?

Washington State Superintendent of Edu-

The chameleon-like SEL adapts to each initiative and capitalizes on every crisis. It rebrands and expands...

---

cation Chris Reykdal recently said the quiet part out loud: "We're changing our literacy standards... students are gonna get age-appropriate learning standards around media literacy...to discern truth from fiction." Such measures risk elevating state-sanctioned "truth" over diverse viewpoints, further consolidating ideological control over public education.

Although formal equity initiatives are being scrapped by Trump's Department of Education, officials should note that some "literacy" efforts align with a DEI agenda that stifles dissent. Vague, overlapping terms form a web of subtle ideological programming – all with the apparent intent to psychologically manage children.

The continual rebranding of "soft skills" – as SEL competencies, 21st Century skills, Common Core standards, "readiness," "resiliency," "durable skills," or even simply as "literacy" – exposes SEL's intent to frame psychological management as academic progress. Whether Dan Goleman knew it or not, his *Emotional Intelligence* vision was the perfect Trojan Horse to groom a technically skilled yet compliant workforce aligned with the globalist mission.

IV. Funding Fervor: How SEL Became Everything to Everyone

Long before DEI needed a facelift, the architects of woke curricula had already had a makeover. In 2001, CASEL ("Collaborative for Academic, Social, and Emotional Learning") swapped "advancement" for "academic" in its acronym, casting SEL as a core educational priority, rather than just a therapeutic add-on. The subtle name change encouraged wider adoption of SEL in schools: A more "academic" SEL appealed to educators, funders, parents, and policymakers alike.

CASEL's 2003 program guide promised even more than emotional regulation and improved academics. It touted SEL as key to "success in school and life." SEL was a policy chameleon that melded with every major education trend of the last quarter century. Its nebulous language adapts easily to fit the funding opportunity.

As American public education continued to struggle, politicians were eager to fund anything that *sounded* like a solution. Conveniently, both the billionaire architects of Common Core and the peddlers of progressive pedagogy found the ultimate financier in Barack Obama.

In his Blueprint for Reform in 2010, President Obama called for "using data to improve students' safety, health, and wellbeing," signaling that forthcoming grants would encourage alignment with new academic standards and digital infrastructure. His "Race to the Top" grants funneled billions to states for so-called College and Career Ready Standards, "school climate" measures, and interoperable student data systems.

In 2011, CASEL rolled out large-scale SEL programs to cities including Austin, Oakland, and Chicago. Peter and Jennifer Buffett's NoVo Foundation supported the effort through the Collaborating Districts Initiative, providing each participating district $250,000 and ongoing support from CASEL consultants.

In 2015, the federal funding floodgates

opened. First, CASEL President Roger P. Weissberg encouraged schools to integrate SEL into other programs, "such as... multi-tiered systems of support, school climate and culture, and discipline." That same year, the Obama administration signed the Every Student Succeeds Act (ESSA) into law, pouring billions into "student supports," school climate and culture, "data-informed decision making," "academic enrichment," and "well-rounded education." Notably, these also included "21st Century Community Learning Centers," extending SEL's reach to after-school care.

Educational software companies were quick to capitalize. As funding and mandates grew, these companies designed tools for digitized SEL. The platforms they built allow schools or districts to parse student data by race, gender, income, or other "lenses" to justify interventions or programmatic changes to boost things like "belonging" or "school climate." For example, a report on Gender-Diverse Students' Experiences in Austin, Texas schools cited its school climate survey to support separate changing spaces for students who identify as "trans" or "nonbinary."

With federal funding flowing through nearly every conceivable channel – academic enrichment, teacher training, workforce training, early interventions, rural students, native students, school safety, mental health, after-school care, and more – ESSA's implementation in 2017-2018 increased K-12 education spending to over $40 billion by 2020.

Beginning in 2020, two crises – the COVID-19 pandemic and the Uvalde, Texas school shooting – were used to justify another surge in SEL spending. The Biden administration's American Rescue Plan (2021) pumped $123 billion into K-12 education. School districts were *required* to reserve 20 percent of it for "evidence-based interventions that respond to the academic, social, and emotional needs of students."

Describing it as an "unprecedented opportunity to invest in SEL," CASEL was now well-positioned as the go-to resource for post-

> *SEL measures and tracks today's children with a precision that would impress George Orwell himself.*

pandemic recovery in education. The following year, the Bipartisan Safer Communities Act (BCSA) earmarked another $1 billion for mental health efforts, including SEL programs to improve — and thus attempt to *measure* — the nebulous concept of "school climate." In explaining the allowable use of BCSA funds, the US Department of Education said it was *critical* for schools to "create a safe place for students and their diverse and intersectional identities."

By 2023, the narrative shifted again. Biden's education department cited a teacher shortage to authorize the use of Perkins Act grants to strengthen the teacher pipeline. Edtech platforms like Xello, YouScience, Schoolinks, and Naviance – marketed "career guidance and academic counseling," full of SEL-aligned workforce development material to help students find their calling as educators.

President Biden's 2024 budget continued the spending on expansive efforts toward "student well-being" and "safe and supportive environments" that often embedded SEL concepts. It proposed another $946 million for mental health efforts – $578 million to increase school-based counselors, psychologists, and social workers, and $368 million to Full-Service Community Schools, which integrate mental health counseling and other medical services including dentists and reproductive health clinics.

The chameleon-like SEL adapts to each initiative and capitalizes on every crisis. It rebrands and expands, co-opting language and taxpayer dollars. Policymakers tout its promises – always urgent enough to fund, but vague enough to evade accountability. All the while, SEL measures and tracks today's children with a precision that would impress George Orwell himself.

V. THE ILLUSION OF CHOICE: THERE IS NO ESCAPE FROM SEL

"There is no escape from such a soul-killing system," warned theologian J. Gresham Machen back in 1922, describing how a state education monopoly would tend toward "pseudoscientific fads of experimental psychology." A century later, families seeking refuge from that monopoly often turn to private schools or to publicly funded alternative schools. But sadly, SEL is not optional. The coveted accreditations of private schools and the "personalized learning" in many charter schools also come with SEL tracking. Virtually every so-called alternative schooling option also embeds SEL, leaving old-fashioned "pencil and paper" instruction as the only way to avoid psychometric profiling. Consider the following examples:

Cognia (formerly AdvancED), the world's largest accreditor of K-12 and post-secondary institutions, bestows its seal of approval on programs teaching 16 million students each year. In 2021, its website proudly declared its commitment to "taking real action toward diversity, equity, and inclusion – in our organization and for our network."

Cognia board member Laura Slover, as discussed above in connection with North Carolina's "Durable Skills" initiative, headed several Gates-funded Common Core entities. Unsurprisingly then, Cognia's K-12 accreditation standards count non-cognitive SEL metrics among its essential criteria for quality education. Alongside traditional academics, Cognia's evaluations also stress "student voice," and "lifelong skills" including curiosity, risk taking, and collaboration.

In a fawning 2023 interview with Cognia VP Jeff Rose, CASEL CEO Aliya Samuel declared SEL an *international* priority and called for *Adult* SEL in the workforce. Cognia's Rose agreed, emphasizing the need to extend SEL "development" to superintendents, principals, and school board members.

National Association of Independent Schools (NAIS)

The "independent" schools accredited by NAIS are far from independent when it comes to DEI compliance and SEL data extraction. In fact, the NAIS created its own system called Data and Analysis for School Leadership to monetize student information. According to its 2021 IRS filings, this database is now NAIS's *largest* source of revenue. The second largest is "equity and justice."

To boost both revenue streams, NAIS offers its Assessment of Inclusivity and Multiculturalism to measure a campus's "climate of inclusivity." This proprietary student survey probes students' personal experiences to ascertain how "safe" and "affirmed" they feel.

Like other SEL tools, the survey is customizable to track the school's progress toward "strategic equity goals."

Video footage leaked from the 2021 NAIS People of Color Conference left no room for doubt: Critical Race Theory was being taught to teachers as foundational to NAIS principles and policies. Former math teacher Paul Rossi was dismissed for speaking out against coercive diversity practices at his NAIS-accredited school. He told *The Wall Street Journal* about a NAIS conference he'd attended: "In '*Small Activists, Big Impact – Cultivating Anti-Racists and Activists in Kindergarten*,' we were told that kindergartners are natural social-justice warriors."

International Baccalaureate Organization

For more than half a century, the International Baccalaureate Organization (IB) has been a leading force in international education, and the "IB" diploma is widely regarded as a badge of academic prestige. But the IB func-

tions as more than just a school accreditor –
it is a transnational mechanism to promote a
values-based worldview through its globally
standardized curriculum.

Founded in 1968 by a former British psychological warfare officer, the IB is a network

---

*"There is no escape from such a
soul-killing system," warned
theologian J. Gresham Machen
back in 1922, describing how a
state education monopoly would
tend toward "pseudoscientific fads
of experimental psychology."*

---

of schools serving 1.95 million students
worldwide. The non-governmental entity
has enjoyed "formal consultive relations" sta-
tus with UNESCO since 1970.

The IB's Primary Years Program promises to develop "academic, social and emotional wellbeing, focusing on international-mindedness." Predictably, "global citizenship" and student activism to fulfill UN Sustainable Development Goals are central themes of IB coursework.

IB students' exams are processed by a proprietary platform called the International Baccalaureate Information System. And in 2020, the IB stressed: "Social and emotional learning (SEL) can and must be incorporated in the curriculum and assessments."

"Big Box" Charter School Networks

Charter schools are a reform innovation of the 1990s. They are independently operated according to a "charter" (contract) between the school's founders and the local or state government. The founders typically lease or build the school, often relying on fundraising, donations, or financing. Its operations are then publicly funded on a per-student basis, similar to traditional (zoned) public schools. Application is open and voluntary, giving rise to the slogan: "Your tax dollars follow your child."

As more states enact charter school laws, Big Tech and Big Philanthropy are leveraging the model to mold young minds at scale. In 2016, the national Project Unicorn initiative, backed by Alphabet (Google), Amazon, Dell, and Microsoft, built on the data infrastructure established under Common Core, accelerating education's shift from "paper and pencil" to cloud-based learning. The result is a vast, interoperable data landscape that allows schools to move budget line items from capital expenditures to operational costs. Thus, was born the data-intensive "big box" charter school chain.

The model is brilliant, if you're a tech billionaire:

> Seed "innovative" schools outfitted with cloud-connected devices.

> Install "data-driven" learning software platforms across the network while promoting "personalized" learning.

> Advocate for "school choice" policies so taxpayers will cover the day-to-day operations, including software subscription fees.

> Sit back and harvest untold terabytes of student data fed to your cloud-based servers each day, at public expense.

This model doesn't just economize school operations, it enables social-emotional profiling, behavioral tracking, and real-time data extraction on a massive scale. School choice advocates like to say "the money follows the student," but in the case of these networks it is more apropos to say the money follows the student's *data* – straight to Silicon Valley.

Charter school networks that use cloud infrastructure in this manner include:

KIPP (Knowledge is Power Program), the largest charter network, tracks the SEL data of more than 190,000 students in 278 schools. KIPP's Character Strengths framework targets psychometric measures like "social intelligence" and "zest." Gates, Walton, Bloomberg, and other tech titans support KIPP.

IDEA (Individuals Dedicated to Excellence and Achievement) network broadcasts daily SEL videos to 87,000 students in 145 schools. MTSS data is tracked by Panorama Education. Its Tier 1 (universal)

For more than three decades, CASEL has woven SEL into every nook and cranny of kids' lives.

SEL instruction follows the DEI-infused "Move this World" curriculum.

XQ Super School Network, founded by Laurene Powell Jobs and former Obama official Russlyn Ali, typifies the data-intensive schooling model. XQ's Student Performance Framework defines student success not by knowledge, but by academic "outcomes" and social-emotional skills.

Summit Schools, a Chan Zuckerberg collaboration, collects SEL data on approximately 4,000 students in California and Washington. The related Summit Learning platform transmits "whole child" (SEL) curricula to more than 200,000 students in partner schools across 43 states.

Career and Technical Education (CTE)

One might assume that vocational education, focused on concrete skills and practical job training, would be a haven from SEL psychometric tracking. It is not. Today's Career and Technical Education (CTE) programs present SEL skills as foundational to workplace success.

A prime example is Advance CTE, a Gates-funded public-private collaboration of state directors and industry partners. Its signature framework, *Career Clusters: Pathways to College & Career Readiness*. The model is graphically depicted by a circle divided into 16 "clusters" or industry sectors defined by the US Department of Education. Within each sector, "career pathways" radiate outward from the center, showing the steps for career development, from general to more specific.

At the very center – the bullseye position and starting point for all 79 career pathways – is "Career Ready Practices." Here, familiar SEL and behavioral traits such as resilience, environmental and social awareness are recast by Advance CTE as "skills needed to succeed in the modern workplace."

Extra *Extracurriculars*

For more than three decades, CASEL has woven SEL into every nook and cranny of kids' lives. It unabashedly calls for "systemic implementation" to go beyond schools and embed SEL into families, communities, and government policies. The sweeping push even includes after-school care and extra-curricular activities.

A 2011 review of after-school programs co-written by CASEL's Roger Weissberg promoted this idea with its "SAFE" (Sequenced, Active, Focused, Explicit) framework – still the go-to method for implementing SEL across settings. Harvard's 2021 Navigating SEL from the Inside Out, endorses not only the SAFE method, but also "Adult SEL" for teachers, and a social justice focus, thereby ensuring that after-school care delivers a daily double-dose of DEI to the children of working parents.

Harvard's guide praises popular after-school programs such as Girls on the Run (a running club) and "Mutt-i-grees" (an SEL program featuring shelter dogs) as exemplars of how to blend physical activities and hobbies with SEL surveys, discussions, and role-play. Meanwhile, even more familiar programs such as Scouting America (formerly Boy Scouts of America), Girl Scouts of America, Boys & Girls Clubs of America, 4-H, and YMCA have also woven SEL into their activities, accepting federal grants to do so through "expanding use of technology," and "enhanc[ed] digital delivery."

Today, kids are subjected to personality quizzes, self-reflection prompts, and empathy exercises not just in school, but also in their free time. The broader implication here is that SEL isn't just embedded in American education. It's part of a much larger push for ideological standardization across families, communities, cultures, and continents.

VI. The Global Infrastructure of SEL

After a decade building the field domestically, CASEL took SEL to the world. The 2004 translation of Goleman's *Emotional Intelligence* into 30 languages helped pave the way for founders and key allies to leverage influence within international entities like UNESCO, the World Economic Forum, and the Organization for Economic Cooperation and Development (OECD).

SEL isn't just embedded in American education. It's part of a much larger push for ideological standardization across families, communities, cultures, and continents.

A key emissary was Linda Darling-Hammond, education advisor to Obama's transition team. Her participation in OECD panels on "21st century competencies," brought worldwide attention to SEL. She contributed to the OECD's "Big Five" personality framework and helped to embed CASEL's model into the OECD's flagship exam, the Programme for International Student Assessment (PISA).

CASEL co-founder Timothy Shriver promoted SEL abroad through his roles at UNESCO, the WEF, Special Olympics International, and the Council on Foreign Relations. Shriver praised SEL as a means to peace, equity, and inclusion, aligning CASEL's concepts to UNESCO's frameworks and the WEF's sustainability agenda.

Dan Goleman and CASEL President Roger Weissberg also advanced SEL globally. Both are widely cited by OECD, the UN, and the WEF. Both helped to position SEL as a means of achieving the UN's Sustainable Development Goals (SDGs). In one

WEF talk, Goleman explicitly pitched Emotional Intelligence (SEL) as "Unlocking your Emotions to Achieve the SDGs."

The convergence of SEL with the UN's sustainability framework was cemented in the mid-2010s. After the "UN Decade of Education for Sustainable Development" (2005-2014), the organization adopted fifteen Sustainable Development Goals, including "Education for Sustainable Development and Global Citizenship. (SDG 4.7)"

By 2019, UNESCO's New Delhi Mahatma Gandhi Institute of Education for Peace and Sustainable Development (MGIEP) had become the UN's SEL nerve center. MGIEP's Global Collective for SEL and Digital Learning engages 37 member organizations to advance SEL for sustainable development. Its mission: to "transform education toward SDG 4.7" through SEL programming.

MGIEP dedicated an entire issue of its magazine *The Blue Dot* to "SEL for SDGs," with features from CASEL President Roger P. Weissberg and others focused on "mindful-

The WHO strategy is, in effect, SEL by yet another name. Across many global initiatives, carefully curated and morphing language hides the ideological effort to reshape individual lives through collective appeal.

ness in education." In the classroom, SEL often takes the form of "reflection" or "mindfulness" activities. The word "mindfulness" appears more than *one hundred times* in the 92-page issue. The UN's "inclusive education practices" encourage daily circle discussions about feelings and social concerns. Confidentiality is emphasized to ensure "authentic" sharing during group sessions.

The progressive vision for an SEL-driven global utopia is clear in UNESCO's 2024 policy guide, Mainstreaming SEL in Education Systems. One SEL case study of 579 primary schools across China concluded, without apparent irony, that "the program's success has garnered widespread praise from society."

The guide goes on to assert that *if* SEL is to "promote social justice within and beyond education" it *must* adhere to the Recommendation on Education for Peace, Human Rights and Sustainable Development. But upon closer review, the *Recommendation* simply restates social justice principles like gender equality and combating 'systemic inequality.' The guide and recommendations together form a circular proposition: for SEL to advance social justice, it must… advance social justice.

Education policy in a growing number of countries similarly invokes this language to justify implementing SEL programs. Major global trade groups in education, from the Association for Supervision and Curriculum Development, to the International Federation of Library Associations, and the International Society for Technology in Education, all profess alignment with the UN agenda.

Collectivism stealthily overtook education by co-opting positive words like "learning" and "literacy," but the pattern repeated across other sectors. As the UN embraced Social Emotional Learning, the World Health Organization (WHO) advanced "Social Determinants of Health." The WHO's Skills for Health framework for public health agencies appeals to "health" – *healthy* relationships, *healthy* reproductive choices, *health* equity, and *healthy* environments–to promote targeted attitudes and "psychosocial competencies." The WHO strategy is, in effect, SEL by yet another name. Across many global initiatives, carefully curated and morphing language hides the ideological effort to reshape individual lives through collective appeal.

VII. Conclusion: Reclaiming Education Through Parent Pushback and Policy Reform

The influence of SEL in education today can hardly be overstated. CASEL psychologists normalized the school-wide assessment of "non-cognitive" traits, reframed them as skills, and inserted them into state standards. Then, cloud-based edtech turbocharged SEL's ability to probe students' minds and subtly shape their worldviews.

To be clear: Educational credits for "social skills" are *social credit*. When education path-

---

Learning is not therapy.
It's time to return to basics:
the pursuit of objective
knowledge.

---

ways are aligned to globalist visions of "equity" and "sustainability," they become tools for control, tying diplomas to ideological conformity. SEL frameworks in all their forms must be recognized as the backbone of a nascent global soft tyranny.

Teachers, no matter how deeply committed to their students, are neither qualified nor authorized to act as therapists or spiritual gurus. And cloud-based "personalized learning" platforms, however effective at teaching math or reading, lack the informed consent of parents to harvest their children's psychometric data. Nonconsensual psychological profiling and interventions have no place in public school classrooms.

The time has come for a reckoning. Grassroots efforts like those of Moms for Liberty and Parents Defending Education are demanding accountability, pushing for parental roles in curriculum review, and challenging SEL's hidden agenda. Several states have passed laws limiting or banning DEI practices, but broader reforms are needed. The 2025 Supreme Court ruling in *Mahmoud v. Taylor* affirms a parent's right to opt their child out of woke curricula – specifically LGBTQ-related lessons – on religious grounds, which could have major implications for SEL programming.

To reorient education towards academic

excellence, Americans must Recognize, Reform, and Retool.

RECOGNIZE. Parents must see through the rhetorical fog of "whole child" education and "workplace-ready" skills. Appealing slogans obscure an agenda that seeks to steer children's beliefs, often in ways that diverge from their family values. Recognizing the ideological foundations of SEL is the first step toward dismantling it.

REFORM. Policymakers must stop SEL psychometric tracking at the source.

> *Curriculum transparency laws must be fully applied to software platforms. Demand local hosting or open-source code from the software creators. Public school learning content should be available for public inspection. Subscription-based software that updates in real time can never be truly transparent.*

> *Opt-In policies: Schools should require explicit, informed parental consent for non-academic*

surveys and assessments. Opt-out policies are invasive because they default to child surveillance if the parent is unaware or fails to take action.

➤ *Defund the Data Harvesters: Lawmakers should stop funding proprietary digital platforms that harvest children's psychometric data or track "social and emotional skills" via adaptive learning modules.*

RETOOL. Educators must get children "out of the cloud." Children too young to give informed consent should learn core academic subjects from physical textbooks or locally hosted software that does not upload their personal data to corporate servers.

Learning is not therapy. It's time to return to basics: the pursuit of objective knowledge. Students should engage with great ideas, study beautiful artwork, music, and literature, and acquire technical and academic skills. These liberal arts are fundamental to individual human freedom and a flourishing society. Let us return education to its rightful purpose and liberate the minds of America's children.

First American edition published in 2025 by Encounter Books,
an activity of Encounter for Culture and Education, Inc.,
a nonprofit, tax-exempt corporation.
Encounter Books website address: www.encounterbooks.com

Manufactured in Canada and printed on
acid-free paper. The paper used in this publication meets
the minimum requirements of ANSI / NISO Z39.48–1992
(R 1997) (*Permanence of Paper*).

FIRST AMERICAN EDITION

Library of Congress Cataloging-in-Publication Data
is available for this title under the ISBN: 978-1-64177-491-8

Sold to parents and teachers as harmless programming for "emotional intelligence," Social Emotional Learning (SEL) became – with the use of cloud-based technology – a centralized apparatus for values transmission that threatens the autonomy of future generations. Through SEL, collectivist propaganda now pervades modern classrooms, shaping your child's worldview, click by click. What started small has become a dangerous subversion of the educational system aimed at surveillance, indoctrination, and, ultimately, compliance with a globalist agenda.

Transparency is their enemy. In this Broadside, Priscilla West exposes SEL as a toxic brew of psychology and sustainability, promoted by an alliance of billionaires, politicians, and consultants at the expense of true education. Only by confronting it can we hold the education-industrial complex accountable and reclaim our schools for authentic learning.

PRISCILLA WEST *is a researcher for Peter Schweizer's Government Accountability Institute and a chapter chair of Moms for Liberty. Her writing reflects a life lived at the intersection of global affairs, community leadership, and chauffeuring of teenagers – with her sense of humor intact.*

$9

$9.99
ISBN 978-1-64177-491-8
5099

9 781641 774918

ENCOUNTER BOOKS

WWW.ENCOUNTERBOOKS.COM